ENCHANTED PRESS
London | New York

Published by Enchanted Press
Copyright © 2023 by
Enchanted Press.

Read by Marina Squierciati
Meditation by
Lynn Sparrow Christy
www.accessyourpotential.net
Illustrated by Nicola Senior
Designed by Collette Sadler

The original concept of the gold
bubble in this story is inspired
by the work and teachings of
Ms Lynette Arkadie,
"The Energy Mentor"
www.myenergymentor.com.
It is used with her permission and
blessing. She hopes that all children
and open-hearted spirits everywhere,
have the power and knowledge to
secure themselves.

First edition published in 2023
by Enchanted Press

ISBN: 978-0-578-33355-7

The artwork in this book is watercolor
with pens and pencils on watercolor
paper.

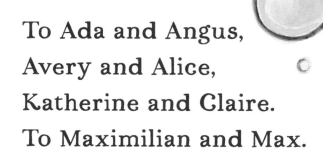

To Ada and Angus,
Avery and Alice,
Katherine and Claire.
To Maximilian and Max.

Adelaide
and the

Cosmic
Rescue Squad

To Sophie ~
I wish you a
magical life! Zoe

Zoe Twitt

Illustrated by Nicola Senior

 **Adelaide** is thrilled because today is **Halloween**.

And Halloween **means**

But **first** she needs a
costume for trick-or-treating.

She climbs the **dusty** stairs to her **attic**

and hauls out an old
wooden trunk.

Inside Adelaide finds a piece of silky pink fabric.
She throws it over her shoulders and voila! A cape.
But wait, there's something at the bottom of the
trunk. It looks like a... **witch's hat**.

Inside the hat is a **message**

written in crayon.

Hubble, nubble,
whizz and bubble,
incant this spell
when you're
in
TROUBLE!

"A real witch's spell!" gasps Adelaide. She spins around and tucks the note carefully into her pocket.

"Let the magic begin!" she squeals,

dashing out the front door and onto Scuttlebug Lane.

Rose is a bag of jellybeans made from multi-colored balloons. She waves to Adelaide!

Aaliyah is looking confident as Madam President of the United States of America. Stretching behind her is a gymnast named **Trinity**.

Imani is an astronaut traveling home from Mars.

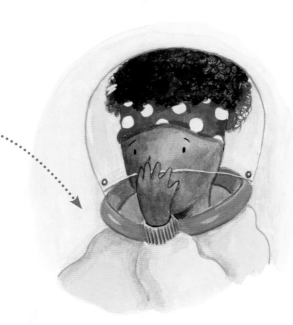

Dressed in her mint green scrubs is **Dr. Mia.** She is ready to perform surgery on Mindy, a patient from her ICU.

The children can't wait to trick-or-treat. **Ina** plays a few chords on her electric guitar to get the party started.

The children squeal
with excitement as
they ring the doorbells
along the lane, shouting,

"Trick-or-treat!"

Adelaide notices the
sun is **dipping**
below the horizon. She starts
to **grow nervous**.
Her stomach hurts. Did she
eat too much candy?

They arrive at the next house.

"It's too dark,"

Adelaide says. The house looks haunted.
Adelaide is certain she sees goblins at the
window. Trinity tucks her blankie around
her shoulders and the children bravely
head down the dark, spooky driveway.

"I'll stay here," Adelaide says shakily

as she watches her friends disappear into the
darkness. Her heart hammers in her chest
and her legs are like wobbly jell-o.

Adelaide puts her hand in her pocket and
touches the curious piece of paper.

Will help really come?

She takes a deep breath
and reads the spell. "Hubble,
nubble, whizz and bubble, incant
this spell when you're in trouble!"

Immediately a bubble of light appears from above. Inside stands a **tiny witchlet**, steering it haphazardly.

Adelaide is
flabbergasted!.

"**Witchlet Zara**, at your service. How can I help you?" The young witch curtsies, her rumpled hat sliding off her head.

Adelaide points at the haunted house and stammers,
"I-I-I'm afraid of the dark."

The witchlet nods, "It feels so **dark** and spooky tonight, doesn't it? Lots of children have called me!"

Witchlet Zara raises her wand, and
with one swish, the haunted house is
filled with **warm lights** and
happy children wave at them
from the window. Adelaide sees her
friends skipping down the driveway
with their bags of candy.

Calista Frederick Diana Amy Joelle Angus Malik Sarah Tyrone Alicia Latonya Razi Leah Tyrell Pippa Oliver Hetty Noah Jacob Alice Sophie Lily Leo

"My work here is **done**," says Zara, "and I have a long list of children in need of some light."

"Wait! Can we help?" offers Aaliyah. "It'll be faster if we all pitch in."

President

"Witchlet Zara agrees. "But you'll need something to drive. **Imagine** a **bubble** around you, all shiny and golden on the outside and cozy on the inside."

The children concentrate.

Adelaide's bubble is the first to appear.

She is bathed in the most **exquisite golden light**. It feels like warmth

and **glitter** and **magic**.

She feels **safe** and **carefree** as she rises into the night sky.

Soon the whole gang is steering their bubbles through the sky, looking like a **cosmic rescue squad**.

They **whoop**

and **wave**

to each other **excitedly**,

ready for

their important

mission.

The first name on the list is Gaby.

The Cosmic Rescue Squad finds her hiding under a bush, **shaking**. "It's too dark out here," she tells them. "I was sure the monsters would get me."

How many more children need help? Witchlet Zara unfolds the list. It's a mile long, and growing before their eyes!

"We need a faster way to rescue all the children!" Adelaide says desperately.

"We need blankies!"

"We need to make a lot of light!"

"We need more magic!"

Without pausing, Adelaide takes a **deep breath**.

She exhales a string of bubbles into the night sky, a glowing string of **golden pearls**.

She blows another, and then

another.

"Then we'll knit our own **blanket!**" Adelaide says.

Mia catches the strands of pearls, curls them around her wrists, and begins to **weave**.

"Everybody, start **knitting!**" Adelaide instructs, tossing two strands to each friend.

It starts out small. A **glowing blanket** of light. It grows quickly and soon it's large enough to drape over Scuttlebug Lane,

then the entire town.

"**Don't stop!**" Aaliyah shouts. The
children keep knitting. The blanket grows
and grows... and **grows** until it

covers all of **planet Earth**.

Looking down, the children admire their work.

"There is so much light" says Gaby. Planet earth is
glowing, wrapped in the light of the magic blanket.

It feels so warm and safe.

Could anyone still be afraid of the dark?

"Zara, do you have the list?"
Adelaide asks. Zara holds it up.
The **page** is **blank**.

Their work is **done**.

Hooray!

"I couldn't have done it without you," Zara tells them. "What we have achieved tonight is **extraordinary**. But now it's past a witchlet's bedtime."

Adelaide sails through her bedroom window. She lands on her bed, feeling the golden blanket float down on her. Deliciously drowsy, she drifts off into a deep and satisfying **sleep**.

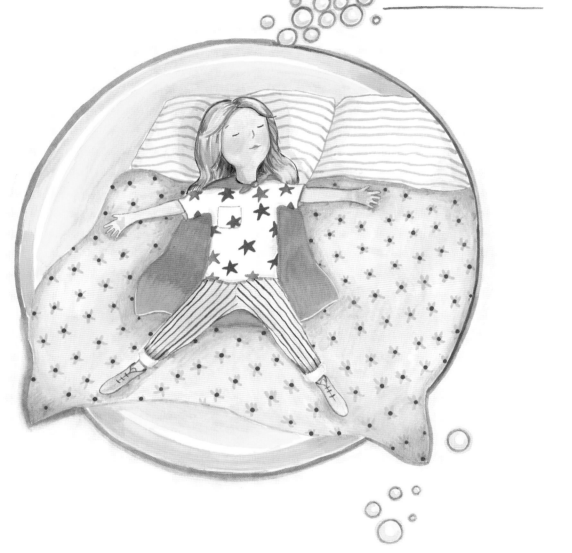

Tonight, when you go to bed, you'll **snuggle down** under the same golden blanket that Adelaide and her friends knitted. Will you join the Cosmic Rescue Squad and knit your own light, when you need it?